SAFETY
LEADERSHIP
ACADEMY

Building Proactive Cultures in High-Stakes
Environments

by
Keric D. Craig, Ed.D.

Dedication

In loving memory of my friend and mentor, Col. Tony Lombardo, whose wisdom, integrity, and example continue to inspire.

To every leader who understands that safety is not compliance but commitment. May this book guide you in building cultures where people return home safely, missions succeed, and organizations thrive.

Preface

Safety is not an accident; it is the result of intentional leadership. Over my career in aerospace and aviation safety systems, I have seen firsthand how organizations succeed when leaders make safety a core value, and how they stumble when safety is reduced to checklists alone. My doctoral work in organizational leadership and development reinforced a truth that I carry into every high-stakes environment: cultures do not change by policy alone. They change when leaders model the behaviors they want to see.

This book is both a guide and a call to action. It is designed as an academy for leaders at every level who are responsible for the lives of others and the success of critical missions. Whether you work in aviation, healthcare, energy, defense, or manufacturing, the principles of proactive safety leadership apply.

About the Author

Keric D. Craig, Ed.D., holds a Doctorate in Organizational Leadership and Development and a master's degree in aerospace/aviation safety systems. He currently serves as a Quality Engineer for one of the leading defense companies in the world, where he applies his expertise in safety systems and organizational leadership to mission-critical programs.

Before transitioning to the defense industry, Dr. Craig served 26 years in the United States Air Force, where he held multiple high-pressure leadership positions, including Nuclear Weapons Superintendent. In these roles, he was entrusted with the management of sensitive operations, the oversight of elite teams, and the maintenance of uncompromising safety standards under the most demanding conditions. His career in uniform provided him with firsthand experience in leading under pressure, shaping resilient organizations, and safeguarding missions of national consequence.

With experience in high-stakes environments, Dr. Craig has dedicated his career to building proactive safety cultures that protect people, advance missions, and sustain organizational excellence. His work bridges leadership theory and practical application, equipping leaders with the tools and values needed to thrive in complex and high-consequence industries.

Table of Contents

Chapter 1:
Introduction – Why Safety Leadership Matters

Every organization in a high-stakes environment faces the same question: How do we ensure safety when failure is not an option? The answer is never just technology, procedure, or compliance. The answer is leadership.

In fields such as aviation, aerospace, healthcare, nuclear power, and defense, safety is often thought of in terms of systems and processes. We build redundant designs, craft detailed checklists, and establish regulations. These safeguards are essential, but they cannot guarantee safety by themselves. History reminds us of this truth. Catastrophic accidents, from aircraft mishaps to industrial explosions, are rarely the result of a single technical failure. They are the outcome of cultural breakdowns: ignored warnings, silenced voices, shortcuts accepted, or leaders who failed to see beyond the checklist.

This is why leadership matters. Technology can reduce risk. Procedures can add discipline. Regulations can create accountability. But only leadership can shape the culture that ensures safety is prioritized, communicated, and lived every day.

Leadership Beyond Compliance

Traditional safety programs often rely heavily on compliance: making sure rules are followed, boxes checked, and audits passed. Compliance is important because it establishes minimum standards and prevents obvious hazards. But in dynamic, high-pressure environments, compliance is not enough. Regulations are reactive by nature; they are created after failures have already occurred.

Proper safety requires more than reaction; it involves anticipation. Leadership moves safety beyond compliance by shaping culture, influencing attitudes, and empowering people

1

to speak up before errors turn into tragedies. A leader's words and actions send powerful signals. When employees see leaders taking shortcuts, they will do the same. When they see leaders pausing to address safety concerns even at the cost of convenience, they learn that safety truly comes first.

A proactive culture, led by leaders who value safety above convenience, creates conditions where hazards are identified early, lessons are shared openly, and accountability is embraced rather than feared. This is where true resilience begins.

The Human Factor

Safety is not only about machines or systems, it is about people. The human factor is both the greatest vulnerability and the greatest asset in high-stakes operations.

A fatigued pilot, a distracted technician, or a disengaged manager can open the door to disaster. History is full of examples: pilots missing critical warnings due to exhaustion, maintenance crews overlooking minor defects under pressure to meet deadlines, or managers suppressing concerns to avoid delays. These errors are rarely malicious; they are often the result of systemic pressures, cultural norms, or inadequate leadership.

Yet the human factor can also be the strongest safeguard. A well-trained, alert, and empowered workforce can detect problems technology misses, adapt in moments of crisis, and prevent accidents before they happen. Leaders determine which version of the human factor dominates their organizations.

Empowered employees are more than rule-followers; they are active participants in safety. They ask questions, report hazards, and intervene when necessary. They believe their voices matter. Creating this environment is not a matter of luck; it is the deliberate work of leaders who prioritize people, listen actively, and encourage accountability without fear.

Lessons from History

The evidence is undeniable: leadership failures often precede organizational tragedies. The Chernobyl nuclear disaster was not simply a technical malfunction but the product of a culture where engineers were pressured to take risks against their judgment. The Deepwater Horizon explosion was not only about mechanical breakdowns but also about leaders dismissing safety warnings in pursuit of speed and profit.

Conversely, examples of strong safety leadership abound. Airlines that embraced Crew Resource Management drastically reduced accidents by empowering every voice in the cockpit. Hospitals that adopted structured safety checklists and servant leadership practices cut surgical errors nearly in half. In both cases, success was not just about tools; it was about leaders shaping the culture in which those tools were used.

A Call to Leaders

This book is about equipping leaders with the tools and mindset to build proactive safety cultures. It is about moving from reactive responses after an accident to proactive prevention long before risks escalate. Leadership in high-stakes environments is not optional; it is decisive.

Leaders must understand that their actions or inactions set the tone for everyone else. Safety is caught more than it is taught; people follow the example they see. If leaders are complacent, teams will mirror complacency. If leaders are vigilant, accountable, and humble, their people will reflect those qualities as well.

The stakes could not be higher. Lives, missions, reputations, and futures depend on leaders who understand that safety is not a department, not a checklist, and not a compliance function; it is a culture. And culture always starts at the top.

This is why safety leadership matters. Because in environments where failure is not an option, leadership is the difference between resilience and catastrophe.

Chapter 2:
Understanding High-Stakes Environments

High-stakes environments are workplaces where the cost of failure is measured not only in dollars but in human lives, mission success, and national security. These are not places where mistakes cause minor inconvenience; they are settings where one decision, one missed signal, or one ignored warning can determine whether people live or die.

To lead effectively in such environments, leaders must first understand what makes them unique and distinct. Leadership in high-stakes organizations is not just about enforcing compliance; it is about cultivating resilience, anticipation, and adaptability among people and systems that constantly operate at the edge of risk.

The Defining Features of High-Stakes Work

High-stakes environments exist across various industries, including aviation, aerospace, nuclear energy, defense, healthcare, oil and gas, as well as critical infrastructure such as power grids and cyber defense. Despite differences, they share common features:

- **Complexity:** Systems contain multiple interdependent parts, technical, human, and organizational. A small misstep can lead to a systemic failure. For example, a single mis-calibrated valve in an oil refinery can trigger an explosion.

- **Time Pressure:** Decisions must often be made in seconds or minutes, with limited information and under intense stress. Leaders must prepare teams to act decisively without complete certainty.

- **Consequence-Heavy Outcomes:** Errors may result in death, mass casualties, environmental disaster, or strategic defeat. In such contexts, "good enough" is never good enough.

- **Visibility and Scrutiny:** Failures are rarely private. They attract public, political, and regulatory attention. Recovery is slow, costly, and often incomplete.

These characteristics mean safety cannot be treated as a checklist; it must be a culture.

The Anatomy of Risk

Every high-stakes environment carries inherent risk. A jet engine can fail in mid-flight. A nuclear reactor can overheat. A surgeon can make a wrong incision. But disasters rarely come from one isolated failure.

The Swiss Cheese Model, developed by James Reason, illustrates how accidents occur when multiple layers of defense fail simultaneously. Each layer has "holes" due to human error, equipment malfunction, and cultural pressures. When the holes align, tragedy occurs. Leaders cannot eliminate all holes, but they can strengthen layers and close gaps before alignment creates catastrophe.

Equally important is the concept of normalization of deviance. Over time, small deviations from standards can become routine if they don't immediately result in harm. This is what happened in NASA's Challenger disaster: foam strikes on the shuttle had occurred before without catastrophic results, leading leaders to accept them as normal. Over time, what was once unacceptable became routine, until disaster struck. Leaders must remain vigilant against this slow erosion of standards.

Case Studies Across Industries
Aviation: Tenerife, 1977

The deadliest aviation disaster in history occurred not from a mechanical breakdown but from communication failures, cultural hierarchies, and pressure. Two 747s collided in heavy fog after miscommunication between air traffic control and the KLM captain. Over 500 lives were lost. The lesson: even in advanced technical systems, culture and communication matter more than technology.

Healthcare: Wrong-Site Surgeries

In hospitals worldwide, wrong-site surgeries have occurred despite the implementation of protocols. These errors happen when communication fails and hierarchies silence junior staff who see mistakes. Institutions that adopted "time out" procedures, empowering all staff to stop the process if they see a risk, dramatically reduced such errors. Leadership set the tone by reinforcing that every voice matters.

Oil & Gas: Deepwater Horizon, 2010

The Gulf of Mexico oil spill demonstrated how leadership culture can magnify risk. Engineers raised concerns about the blowout preventer, but management ignored warnings to save time and money. The result: 11 lost lives, billions in damage, and irreparable environmental harm. This was not a technical failure alone; it was a leadership failure to prioritize safety over production.

Nuclear Energy: Fukushima, 2011

Following a massive earthquake and tsunami, cooling systems failed at the Fukushima Daiichi nuclear plant. Investigations revealed that leaders had ignored warnings about vulnerability to natural disasters. A culture of denial and deference prevented corrective action. The event prompted a global reevaluation of nuclear safety leadership.

The Human Dimension

Technology can only do so much. People are the most unpredictable factor in high-stakes environments. Fatigue, stress, distraction, overconfidence, and groupthink all undermine performance. Yet people are also the greatest defense. Humans can adapt, improvise, and recognize weak signals long before machines can.

Leaders determine which side of human nature dominates:

- In a toxic culture, people hide mistakes, cut corners, and fear speaking up.
- In a healthy culture, people feel empowered, valued, and accountable.
- Servant leaders shift the balance toward the latter by:
- Respecting limits (ensuring adequate rest, recognizing stress).
- Valuing every perspective, not just senior voices.
- Encouraging reporting without punishment.
- Protecting psychological safety so employees act as sentinels, not silent bystanders.

The Cost of Failure

The consequences of failure extend far beyond the immediate event:

1. **Human Cost:** Lives lost, families broken, communities scarred.
2. **Organizational Cost:** Trust destroyed, missions delayed, reputations tarnished.
3. **Societal Cost:** Public confidence eroded, industries disrupted, regulations tightened, and taxpayer trust diminished.

These costs illustrate why safety leadership is not just an operational priority but a moral obligation.

Anticipation, Not Reaction

The best leaders in high-stakes environments think beyond compliance. They ask: What could go wrong? How do we prevent it before it occurs?

Reactive leaders depend on investigations after failures. Proactive leaders create early-warning systems, encourage hazard reporting, and look for weak signals. They recognize that silence is the enemy of safety and that cultivating vigilance is the highest form of leadership.

Reflection Questions for Leaders

At the end of this chapter, consider the following:

Q1 Do I truly understand the complexity of my environment, or do I oversimplify risks?

Q2, Am I encouraging my team to share weak signals and near-misses?

Q3, Have I examined where "normalization of deviance" may be creeping into our practices?

Q4, Do I balance technical excellence with cultural vigilance?

Q5, Am I serving my people by protecting them from fatigue, pressure, or silence?

Looking Ahead

Understanding the unique pressures and risks associated with high-stakes environments is the foundation of effective safety leadership. The next chapter explores how organizational safety has evolved, shifting from compliance-driven approaches that focused on reacting to accidents to modern proactive models that place leadership and culture at the center of resilience.

Chapter 3:
The Evolution of Organizational Safety

Safety leadership has not always looked the way it does today. The frameworks, tools, and cultural models we rely on in high-stakes environments have been forged through trial, error, and tragedy. To understand how we arrived at modern concepts such as Safety Management Systems (SMS) and High Reliability Organizations (HROs), leaders must look back at the evolution of safety itself.

History shows us that safety improvements rarely happen by choice; they are born out of necessity. Disasters, lawsuits, and public outrage have often been the catalysts for reform. The challenge for leaders today is to learn from these lessons without waiting for failure to strike their own organizations.

From Compliance to Commitment

In the early industrial era, safety was an afterthought. Factories, mines, and railroads were built to maximize production and profit. Workers were considered expendable. Injuries and fatalities were common, often accepted as "the cost of doing business."

Governments eventually responded with regulations and basic rules designed to reduce the most obvious hazards. Hard hats, guards on machines, fire exits, and later, agencies like OSHA in the United States, introduced standards that set minimum requirements for safety.

This compliance model marked an important step forward, but it had its limitations. Regulations are inherently reactive; they are written after an accident has already occurred. Organizations focused on "meeting the standard," but rarely went beyond it. Safety became about checking boxes, not building cultures.

Leaders at this stage often saw safety as someone else's job, a department, an inspector, or a compliance officer. What was missing was recognition that leadership itself is the most important safety system.

Systems Thinking and Human Factors

By the mid-20th century, as industries became more complex, leaders and researchers began to recognize that accidents could not be explained solely by individual errors. Instead, failures were the result of system breakdowns.

This insight gave rise to systems thinking, a perspective that examines how people, processes, technology, and culture interact with one another. The "Swiss Cheese Model," introduced by psychologist James Reason, demonstrated that accidents occur when multiple layers of defense fail at the same time. Each layer has weaknesses in design, human error, and cultural complacency, but when these holes align, disaster results.

Equally important was the growth of human factors research. Experts discovered that errors were often the result of predictable human limitations: fatigue, distraction, overconfidence, stress, or poor design of controls and interfaces. Blaming workers was no longer sufficient. Leaders needed to redesign systems that accounted for human realities.

The Birth of Safety Management Systems (SMS)

Nowhere was this evolution clearer than in aviation. In the late 20th century, accident investigations revealed that compliance with regulations was not enough to prevent disasters. Many organizations were technically "safe" on paper, but culture told a different story.

In response, regulators and industry leaders developed Safety Management Systems (SMS), a proactive approach to embedding safety into an organization's DNA. SMS is built on four pillars:

1. Safety Policy – Leadership commitment to safety as a core organizational value.

2. Safety Risk Management – Identifying, assessing, and mitigating hazards before they cause harm.
3. Safety Assurance – Continuously monitoring and improving safety performance.
4. Safety Promotion – Communicating, training, and fostering a positive safety culture.

Unlike compliance-based models, SMS requires leadership engagement. A policy written on paper is meaningless unless leaders actively model it, reinforce it, and allocate resources to make it real.

High Reliability Organizations (HROs)

As researchers studied organizations that consistently operated safely despite enormous risks such as nuclear power plants, aircraft carriers, and air traffic control centers, they discovered common traits. These organizations became known as High Reliability Organizations (HROs).

HROs succeed not because they eliminate errors but because they are relentlessly vigilant. They operate with five defining principles:

1. Preoccupation with Failure – Treating small errors and anomalies as warnings of larger risks.
2. Reluctance to Simplify – Avoiding oversimplified explanations and digging deeper into root causes.
3. Sensitivity to Operations – Maintaining constant awareness of frontline realities.
4. Commitment to Resilience – Building capacity to adapt and recover quickly when things go wrong.
5. Deference to Expertise – Allowing the most knowledgeable person, not just the highest-ranking, to make critical decisions.

For leaders, HRO principles underscore humility. Servant leaders in HROs recognize that they don't have all the answers.

They listen, defer to expertise, and foster environments where learning is a constant process.

The Role of Servant Leadership in This Evolution

The thread running through the evolution of safety is the role of leadership. Regulations and systems provide structure, but leadership provides culture. And the most effective leaders in high-stakes environments are servant leaders.

- In the compliance era, leaders who cared about people were often the only ones driving improvements beyond the minimum.
- In the systems era, servant leaders embraced human factors by acknowledging human limitations and designing systems to support, not punish, people.
- In SMS and HRO models, servant leaders are indispensable. They promote psychological safety, encourage reporting, and ensure that expertise is valued over hierarchy.

Without servant leadership, SMS becomes merely paperwork, and HRO principles remain theoretical. With servant leadership, they become living, breathing practices that transform organizations.

Historical Lessons

Several disasters illustrate what happens when leadership fails to evolve:

- Challenger (1986): Engineers warned of O-ring risks in cold temperatures, but leadership dismissed their concerns. A culture of schedule pressure overrode safety.
- Columbia (2003): Foam strikes during launch had been normalized. Leaders minimized concerns and silenced dissent, leading to the shuttle's destruction.

- Piper Alpha Oil Platform (1988): A gas leak and subsequent explosion killed 167 workers. Investigations revealed poor communication, inadequate training, and leadership failures in emergency planning.

These tragedies underscore that compliance, technology, and systems cannot substitute for leadership.

From Reaction to Proactivity

The evolution of organizational safety reveals a shift from reactive to proactive approaches:

- Reactive Safety (Pre-1960s): Accidents happen, rules follow.
- Compliance Safety (1960s–1980s): Regulations enforced, but culture often ignored.
- Systems Safety (1980s–1990s): Recognition of complexity and human factors.
- Proactive Safety (2000s–present): SMS, HRO principles, and culture-driven leadership.

This trajectory shows progress but also responsibility. Leaders today inherit the lessons of history. They cannot claim ignorance of the role culture and leadership play in safety.

Reflection Questions for Leaders

Q1, Am I treating safety as compliance or as culture?

Q2, Do I design systems that account for human strengths and limitations?

Q3, Do I encourage reporting of small anomalies as opportunities to learn?

Q4, Do I rely on rank for decision-making, or do I defer to expertise?

Q5, Am I modeling the evolution of leadership by serving my people first?

Looking Ahead

The evolution of safety has brought us to a crucial truth: culture is the ultimate safety system. In the next chapter, we will explore how leadership acts as the catalyst of culture, turning policies into behaviors and shaping the invisible system that determines whether organizations thrive or fail.

Chapter 4:
Leadership as the Catalyst

Every organization has policies, procedures, and safeguards, but only leadership can turn those tools into a living culture of safety. Leadership is the catalyst that transforms written rules into practiced behaviors and aspirational values into daily habits. Without leaders who embody safety, even the most advanced systems will eventually erode under the pressures of time, stress, and competing priorities.

Proper safety does not live in a binder or an audit checklist; it lives in people. And it is leadership that sparks and sustains that life.

Leaders vs. Managers

It is essential to distinguish between managers of safety and leaders of safety. Managers enforce rules, monitor compliance, and track metrics. Their role is critical, without systems of accountability, safety drifts into chaos. Yet management alone is insufficient.

Leaders, by contrast, move beyond enforcement to inspiration. They model the behaviors they expect, create meaning behind the rules, and foster environments where individuals feel a personal stake in safety outcomes. While managers say, "Follow this procedure because it is required," leaders say, "Follow this procedure because it protects your teammates, your family, and your future."

In high-stakes environments, such as hospitals, nuclear plants, aircraft cockpits, or military operations, leadership is essential for producing proactive cultures. These are places where employees wait to be told what to do, hesitate to speak up, and suppress instincts when danger looms. Leadership transforms that passivity into active commitment, shifting the mindset from blind compliance to shared ownership.

Servant Leadership: A Model for Safety

Among the many leadership models, Servant Leadership is uniquely powerful in shaping enduring safety cultures. Introduced by Robert K. Greenleaf, this model reframes leadership not as command, but as service. A servant leader exists to support their people, not to be elevated above them.

In the context of safety, servant leaders embody these principles:

- Prioritize people over processes. They know that protecting human lives is more important than hitting production quotas or timelines.
- Listen first. They create space for feedback, encourage hazard reporting, and amplify voices that might otherwise go unheard.
- Empower teams. By distributing authority, they enable the person closest to a hazard to act decisively, rather than waiting for permission.
- Model humility. When leaders admit mistakes, seek advice, and learn openly, they normalize honesty, making it safe for others to do the same.

Servant leadership transforms safety from a top-down directive into a shared mission. People are far more likely to embrace safe practices when they know their leaders genuinely care about their well-being.

Trust and Psychological Safety

Trust is the foundation of every effective safety culture, and servant leaders are trust-builders by nature. When trust takes root, psychological safety follows the belief that one can speak up, ask questions, or point out risks without fear of ridicule or punishment.

Research across various industries reveals that teams with high psychological safety consistently outperform those without it, particularly under stressful conditions. In aviation, for instance, co-pilots who feel safe to challenge a captain's decision have prevented countless accidents. In contrast, leaders who punish mistakes or silence dissent destroy the very conditions that make accidents preventable.

Servant leaders use errors as opportunities to learn, not to shame. This approach does not lower standards; rather, it reinforces a culture where vigilance is shared, risks are surfaced early, and resilience grows stronger with each lesson learned.

The Ripple Effect of Leadership

Leadership behaviors cascade through organizations. A single leader's daily choices, whether to cut a corner or to pause for safety, send signals that ripple outward. When leaders consistently model humility, care, and commitment to safety, those values spread across teams, departments, and eventually the entire organization.

Conversely, when leaders dismiss concerns, prioritize output over safety, or ignore small violations, those behaviors are quickly imitated. In high-stakes environments, where the consequences of failure are magnified, this ripple effect is decisive. One leader's courage can protect hundreds of lives, while one leader's negligence can endanger them all.

Case Studies: Leadership in Crisis
Tenerife Airport Disaster (1977)

The deadliest accident in aviation history occurred when two Boeing 747s collided on the runway in Tenerife, killing 583 people. Investigations revealed that rigid hierarchy and lack of psychological safety were major contributors. The captain of one aircraft, a highly respected senior pilot, initiated takeoff without clearance. Junior crew members suspected something was wrong, but hesitated to challenge him directly. Their silence, shaped by a culture where questioning authority was discouraged, proved fatal.

This tragedy became a turning point for aviation, leading to the development of Crew Resource Management (CRM) training, which emphasizes servant-leader behaviors, including encouraging open communication, flattening hierarchies in the cockpit, and empowering all voices to speak up.

Chernobyl Nuclear Disaster (1986)

At the Chernobyl nuclear power plant, a late-night safety test spiraled into the worst nuclear accident in history. A toxic mix of poor leadership, secrecy, and authoritarian culture created conditions for catastrophe. Operators followed unsafe instructions, ignored warning signs, and silenced dissent. Managers prioritized meeting political expectations over protecting workers and communities. The absence of servant leadership leaders willing to listen, question, and prioritize human life magnified a technical failure in a global disaster.

Chernobyl illustrates the opposite of servant leadership: a culture where fear and control replace trust and service. The lesson is clear: when leadership suppresses honesty and humility, the cost is measured in life.

Servant Leaders in Action

Examples of servant leadership in safety-critical fields are powerful reminders of its impact:

- Aviation: Captains who actively encourage co-pilots and flight attendants to voice concerns to prevent accidents that might otherwise go unnoticed.
- Healthcare: Surgeons who model humility and invite input from nurses and technicians create surgical teams that catch errors before they become irreversible.
- Military: Commanders who put the welfare of their troops above personal prestige foster units that remain resilient and mission-ready, even under extreme pressure.

- Energy and Manufacturing: Plant managers who walk the floor, engage workers directly, and act swiftly on reported hazards prevent both minor injuries and catastrophic failures.

In each case, servant leadership amplifies the qualities of vigilance, courage, and accountability that save lives and sustain organizations.

The Leader's Responsibility

Ultimately, leaders carry the responsibility for shaping culture. Systems and procedures may provide a framework, but leaders animate them. They set the tone, reinforce the values, and cultivate the conditions where safety can thrive.

In high-stakes environments, this responsibility cannot be delegated. Leaders must serve, protect, and guide. They must be the first to model the behaviors they expect and the last to compromise safety for convenience.

The message is clear: leaders who serve their people build organizations that endure. Servant leadership is not merely a philosophy; it is a practical strategy for building proactive safety cultures where lives are valued above all else.

Looking Ahead

With leadership as the catalyst, culture becomes the vehicle for achieving lasting safety. Policies and procedures may provide structure, but culture determines whether they are effectively implemented or ignored. In the next chapter, we will explore how culture functions as the invisible safety system, shaping decisions and behaviors long before an accident occurs.

Chapter 5:
Culture: The Invisible Safety System

When leaders step into their roles, they inherit more than policies and procedures. They inherit a culture, a set of shared beliefs, norms, and unwritten rules that silently govern how people behave. In high-stakes environments, culture functions as the invisible safety system. It determines whether procedures are followed when no one is watching, whether hazards are reported when it is uncomfortable, and whether safety is treated as a priority or a burden.

Culture is not written in manuals, but it is written in habits. It is not found in audits, but in conversations between workers. And while systems and technology may provide layers of protection, culture decides whether those protections are used, ignored, or quietly bypassed.

What Is Culture?

Culture is not a slogan on a wall or a policy in a handbook. It is what people do day to day, the unwritten rules that guide behavior when no one is keeping score.

- In organizations with strong safety cultures, employees take ownership of identifying hazards, leaders respond quickly and transparently, and everyone feels responsible for the well-being of others.
- In weak cultures, silence prevails, shortcuts are normalized, and safety becomes secondary to production pressures.

For example, after the Exxon Valdez oil spill in 1989, investigators found more than technical failures. They uncovered a culture where fatigue was tolerated, concerns were ignored, and procedures were inconsistently applied. Contrast this with NASA's shift after the Apollo 1 fire in 1967, where leadership rebuilt culture around openness and rigorous testing changes that helped land astronauts safely on the Moon only two years later.

Culture, therefore, is the invisible system that can either shield organizations from disaster or steer them toward it.

The Role of Leadership in Shaping Culture

Culture always reflects leadership. Leaders send signals through their actions, consistency, and priorities that tell employees what truly matters.

- If leaders cut corners, employees learn that speed outweighs safety.
- If leaders listen and act on concerns, employees learn that safety is valued above all else.
- If leaders are inconsistent, culture becomes confused and fragmented.

This is why servant leadership is so powerful in shaping culture. Leaders who prioritize people over processes build trust, and trust becomes the foundation of resilience. When a leader admits mistakes, encourages openness, and serves others, they create an environment where safety is not imposed but embraced.

Culture is not taught in a single workshop; it is absorbed through repeated observation of what leaders reward, tolerate, and ignore.

The "Just Culture" Model

One of the most effective frameworks for strengthening safety cultures is the Just Culture model. Unlike blame-driven models that punish all mistakes, a just culture distinguishes between three behaviors:

- **Human Error:** Unintentional mistakes, slips, or lapses.
- **At-Risk Behavior:** Taking shortcuts, often without fully realizing the risk.

- **Reckless Behavior:** Conscious disregard for safety or rules.

In a just culture:

- Human error is met with understanding, support, and systemic improvement, not punishment.
- At-risk behaviors are addressed with coaching and education, helping people see the risks they missed.
- Reckless behavior is the only category that warrants discipline.

This balance creates accountability while preserving trust. It encourages workers to report problems early, knowing they won't be unfairly blamed for being human. Aviation's adoption of just culture principles, for example, transformed reporting systems. Pilots and crews now routinely submit hazard reports that prevent accidents, because they trust the system will treat them fairly.

Culture as a Preventive System

Strong cultures prevent accidents long before they happen. They encourage proactive reporting, foster open communication, and reinforce vigilance. In this sense, culture is like an early-warning radar, detecting faint signals of danger before disaster strikes.

Weak cultures, however, magnify risks. Hazards go unreported, workers stay silent, and leaders remain unaware until it is too late. The Columbia Space Shuttle disaster (2003) is a sobering example. Engineers raised concerns about foam damage to the shuttle's wing, but cultural pressures to stay on schedule silenced those warnings. Technical failure played a role, but culture ultimately proved to be the deciding factor.

When culture fails, even the best safety systems collapse. When culture is strong, even imperfect systems can be rescued by human vigilance.

Culture Is Local and Organizational

Culture exists on multiple levels. Overall organization may promote safety, but local cultures within teams, departments, or worksites often determine day-to-day behavior.

- A corporate mission statement may emphasize safety, but a single team leader who prizes speed over caution can undo those efforts.
- A hospital may have policies for patient safety, yet if one surgical unit tolerates shortcuts, the risk to patients increases dramatically.

Leaders must therefore be attentive not only to organizational culture but also to local subcultures. This requires walking the floor, engaging directly with employees, and paying attention to small signals of cultural drift.

Building and Sustaining Culture

Building a strong safety culture is an intentional, long-term effort. It requires consistent practices such as:

- **Modeling behavior:** Leaders must embody the values they expect, even when inconvenient.
- **Reinforcing expectations:** Storytelling, rituals, and recognition embed safety into the daily fabric of work.
- **Encouraging participation:** Employees should be treated as partners, not passive followers.
- **Responding to issues:** Swift, transparent responses to hazards and incidents build credibility.

But culture is not a "set and forget" system. It requires vigilance and renewal. Complacency is culture's greatest enemy. Sustaining culture means refreshing training, learning from near misses, and adapting to new challenges such as automation, emerging technologies, or changing workforce dynamics.

The Invisible Becomes Visible

Though culture is invisible, its impact is visible in every decision and outcome. It shows itself when:

- Workers pause to double-check a critical step, even under time pressure.
- A junior employee feels empowered to stop a process because something seems unsafe.
- Teams celebrate success in ways that reinforce and do not compromise safety.

Culture is the thread that connects small daily choices to major organizational outcomes. In high-stakes environments, it is often the difference between resilience and disaster.

Looking Ahead

With culture established as the invisible safety system, the next step is communication of the lifeblood of proactive cultures. Strong cultures thrive on strong communication: without it, trust erodes, silence grows, and risks multiply. Chapter 6 will examine how leaders can build communication systems that foster trust, transparency, and accountability in high-stakes environments.

Chapter 6:
Communication in High-Stakes Settings

Communication is the lifeblood of safety. No system, checklist, or policy can prevent accidents if people fail to share information effectively. In high-stakes environments where seconds matter and consequences are severe, clear, honest, and timely communication can be the difference between success and catastrophe.

Communication is not just a technical process. It is a leadership discipline, a cultural signal, and a human lifeline. When it breaks down, even the best-designed systems crumble.

Why Communication Matters Most

Every major safety incident includes a breakdown in communication. A warning not shared, a concern dismissed, a signal misinterpreted, these gaps are often the weak link in otherwise well-engineered systems.

- At NASA's Challenger disaster (1986), engineers expressed concern about the O-ring seals in cold weather. Their warnings were filtered, softened, and ultimately ignored in communication up the chain. The shuttle launched and exploded.

- In contrast, Captain "Sully" Sullenberger's Miracle on the Hudson (2009) demonstrated the opposite: rapid, clear, structured communication between captain, co-pilot, air traffic controllers, and crew turned a catastrophe into a survival story for 155 passengers.

These examples reveal the truth: communication is not just about information exchange; it is about creating understanding, alignment, and trust.

Barriers to Effective Communication

Several barriers prevent strong communication in high-stakes organizations:

- Hierarchy: Junior team members may hesitate to challenge authority.
- Fear of blame: Employees may hide errors to avoid punishment.
- Information overload: Too much data can bury critical signals.
- Cultural differences: Global teams may interpret tone and meaning differently.
- Stress and fatigue: Under pressure, clarity and attention decline.

These barriers are not theoretical; they shape daily decisions. In healthcare, for example, nurses often report hesitating to question a senior surgeon even when they see a mistake. In aviation, copilots once avoided contradicting captains for fear of reprimand.

Servant leadership helps remove these barriers. By listening actively, inviting input, and valuing every voice, servant leaders flatten hierarchies and reduce fear, making communication more open and effective.

Transparency and Feedback Loops

A proactive safety culture requires transparency. Leaders must share both successes and failures openly, demonstrating that safety is a shared responsibility. Transparency builds credibility: when employees see leaders' own mistakes and address issues directly, they are more likely to report concerns themselves.

Equally critical are feedback loops. Reporting systems must not only collect information but also respond. If an employee submits a hazard report and hears nothing back, trust is eroded. But if leaders acknowledge the input, act on it, and communicate the outcome, trust deepens.

Closed feedback loops create a reinforcing cycle: reporting leads to action, action leads to improvement, and improvement strengthens reporting. This loop is the heartbeat of continuous safety communication.

Lessons from Aviation and Healthcare

Two fields, aviation and healthcare, offer powerful lessons on the role of structured communication.

- Aviation: The adoption of Crew Resource Management (CRM) was revolutionary. CRM emphasized that everyone on the crew, regardless of rank, had the duty to speak up when they saw danger. Captains were trained to invite input, and copilots were empowered to challenge decisions. Countless accidents have been prevented because communication shifted from silent deference to active dialogue.

- Healthcare: Borrowing from aviation, healthcare introduced structured communication tools such as the surgical "time out." Before a procedure, the entire team pauses to confirm the patient, procedure, and plan. This deliberate check has prevented wrong-site surgeries and saved lives.

The lesson is clear: communication systems must be structured, practiced, and reinforced until they become second nature.

Creating Psychological Safety Through Communication

Communication thrives when employees feel safe to speak. Leaders must create psychological safety, the belief that no one will be punished or humiliated for raising concerns.

Servant leaders foster this environment by:

- Actively asking for input rather than waiting for it.
- Thanking employees who raise issues, even when inconvenient.

- Modeling vulnerability by admitting their own mistakes.
- Protecting whistleblowers and truth-tellers from retaliation.

When people know their voices matter, communication shifts from reactive to proactive. Hazards surface early, near misses are shared, and systemic improvements follow.

Communication in Crisis

In emergencies, communication must be both fast and accurate. Ambiguity kills; clarity saves.

- Standardized language: Using clear, agreed-upon terms reduces misinterpretation.
- Structured briefings: Quick but organized updates ensure shared understanding.
- Redundant confirmation: Critical instructions are repeated back to confirm accuracy.

In the 1989 crash of United Airlines Flight 232, the crew's calm, structured communication allowed them to coordinate an unprecedented partial landing after total hydraulic failure. While lives were tragically lost, the survival of 185 passengers was a testament to disciplined crisis communication.

At the same time, leaders must model composure. Panic spreads quickly, but so does calmness. Leaders who communicate with steadiness and clarity anchor their teams, enabling decisive action under extreme pressure.

Communication as a Leadership Discipline

Leaders cannot delegate communication. They must practice it daily through safety briefings, after-action reviews, walkarounds, and informal conversations. Every interaction is an opportunity to reinforce values, clarify expectations, and strengthen trust.

- Daily check-ins show attentiveness.
- After-action reviews turn mistakes into learning opportunities.
- Informal conversations build relational trust, making formal communication easier when the stakes rise.

Over time, consistent communication builds a culture where information flows freely, risks are identified early, and teams operate with unity.

Looking Ahead

Communication is the mechanism by which leadership and culture come alive. Without it, leadership intentions are never understood, and culture remains unspoken. With it, organizations develop resilience, agility, and trust.

The next chapter will present the Safety Leadership Academy framework, outlining the core competencies leaders must master to build proactive safety cultures across industries.

Chapter 7:
The Academy Model Explained

The purpose of this book is not only to inspire leaders to value safety but also to provide a practical framework for building proactive safety cultures. The Safety Leadership Academy provides that framework. It is designed as a structured pathway for developing leaders who understand that safety is not just a program or compliance checklist; it is a way of leading, thinking, and serving others.

The Academy is not about theory for its own sake. It is about building habits, shaping mindsets, and instilling the competencies that allow leaders to protect lives, sustain trust, and guide organizations through uncertainty.

Why an Academy?

The word *academy* implies structured learning, guided development, and intentional growth. In high-stakes environments, safety leadership cannot be left to chance or assumed to emerge naturally. Leaders must be trained, mentored, and equipped with the skills necessary to lead effectively in high-pressure situations.

An academy approach ensures:

- **Consistency:** Every leader, regardless of background, receives a shared foundation.
- **Accountability:** Progress is tracked, and expectations are clear.
- **Sustainability:** Lessons are not one-time events but a developmental journey.
- **Cultural Transformation:** As more leaders are developed, the culture shifts from reactive compliance to proactive ownership.

Just as pilots go through flight academies and surgeons through residency programs, safety leadership requires an intentional developmental process.

Core Competencies of Safety Leaders

The Academy identifies six core competencies that every leader must master. These competencies form the DNA of proactive safety leadership.

1. **Servant Leadership**
   o *Placing people first:* Prioritizing human life and well-being over deadlines or metrics.
   o *Empowering teams:* Distributing authority so those closest to hazards have the confidence and backing to act.
   o *Practical example:* A plant manager halts production when workers identify a hazard, signaling that people matter more than output.

2. **Systems Thinking**
   o *Seeing the big picture:* Understanding how human, technical, and organizational factors interact.
   o *Preventing blind spots:* Recognizing that accidents rarely have a single cause but emerge from complex systems.
   o *Practical example:* An airline safety leader mapping how scheduling pressures, crew fatigue, and weather combine to create risk.

3. **Communication Mastery**
   o *Clarity under pressure:* Practicing structured communication that eliminates ambiguity.
   o *Building trust:* Establishing feedback loops and transparency so employees know their voices matter.
   o *Practical example:* A surgical team calling a "time out" to confirm patient and procedure, preventing catastrophic error.

4. **Decision-Making Under Pressure**
   - *Balancing speed and thoughtfulness:* Making timely, ethical, and informed decisions under time constraints.
   - *Prioritizing values over expedience:* Choosing safety even when operational or financial pressures compete.
   - *Practical example:* A military commander delaying a mission due to unsafe conditions, despite external pressure to proceed.

5. **Cultural Stewardship**
   - *Living the values:* Leaders modeling the behaviors they expect.
   - *Sustaining vigilance:* Reinforcing safety rituals, norms, and rewards daily.
   - *Practical example:* Leaders start every meeting with a safety moment, embedding vigilance into the organizational rhythm.

6. **Learning Orientation**
   - *Turning mistakes into lessons:* Using incidents and near misses as opportunities for organizational growth.
   - *Encouraging adaptability:* Preparing teams to evolve as environments and risks change.
   - *Practical example:* A hospital using a near miss as a case study in training sessions to prevent future harm.

Training Modules in the Academy

The Academy curriculum is delivered through progressive modules, each designed to strengthen one or more of the core competencies:

- **Module 1:** Foundations of Servant Leadership Leaders learn to serve rather than command, practicing humility, listening, and prioritizing human dignity.

- **Module 2:** Systems Thinking and Human Factors Participants study famous failures (e.g., Chernobyl, Columbia Shuttle) to understand how small oversights cascade into disasters.
- **Module 3:** Communication in High-Stakes Environments
  Leader's practice structured communication techniques such as SBAR (Situation, Background, Assessment, Recommendation), aviation-style callouts, and feedback loop design.
- **Module 4:** Decision-Making Under Stress Through simulations, case studies, and crisis drills, leaders develop judgment and composure in time-sensitive situations.
- **Module 5:** Building and Sustaining Culture Focuses on rituals, recognition systems, and leadership consistency that embed safety into the "way we do things."
- **Module 6:** Continuous Learning and Resilience Emphasizes after-action reviews, continuous improvement cycles, and building resilience into teams and organizations.

These modules are not abstract lessons but immersive, applied learning experiences that translate directly into field practice.

The Role of Mentorship and Coaching

No academy succeeds through curriculum alone. The true transformation occurs through mentorship and coaching.

- Experienced leaders must model servant leadership daily.
- Coaches guide new leaders through real challenges, reinforcing principles with lived wisdom.
- Peer-to-peer mentorship creates a community of accountability and shared growth.

In this way, the Academy becomes more than a classroom; it becomes a living community of practice, where leadership is demonstrated as much as it is taught.

Accountability and Measurement

The Academy must measure outcomes to ensure effectiveness. Metrics should move beyond compliance checklists and focus on cultural health.

Examples of leading indicators include:

- Frequency and quality of hazard reporting.
- Employee engagement and trust survey results.
- Observed behaviors during drills and real operations.
- Near-miss reporting rates (which typically rise in strong cultures).

Accountability also means personal growth. Leaders must be evaluated not only on their results but also on how they achieve them, considering whether their behaviors align with servant leadership and cultural stewardship.

From Framework to Practice

The Safety Leadership Academy is not theoretical. It is a practical, actionable framework for any high-stakes environment, such as aviation, healthcare, defense, manufacturing, or energy.

By mastering servant leadership, systems thinking, communication, decision-making, cultural stewardship, and learning orientation, leaders develop the competencies that prevent accidents, sustain trust, and build resilience.

When practiced consistently, the Academy becomes more than a program. It becomes a movement that transforms safety from a policy into a living value.

Looking Ahead

Now that the Academy model has been outlined, the next chapter will provide tools and frameworks that bring these competencies to life. These include proven strategies such as the PDCA cycle, Safety Management Systems (SMS), and the principles of High-Reliability Organizations (HROs), which are practical methods that turn leadership values into daily operational reality.

Chapter 8:
Tools and Frameworks for Proactive Safety

Principles and leadership values provide the foundation of safety, but leaders also need practical tools to bring those values to life. The Safety Leadership Academy equips leaders with proven frameworks that support the development of proactive safety cultures across various industries. These tools are not theoretical; they have been tested in aviation, defense, healthcare, energy, and other high-stakes environments where failure is not an option.

Frameworks such as the PDCA Cycle, Safety Management Systems (SMS), and High Reliability Organization (HRO) principles provide leaders with the structure to translate values into daily practice. When combined with servant leadership, they become more than systems; they become powerful engines for resilience.

The PDCA Cycle: Driving Continuous Improvement

The Plan-Do-Check-Act (PDCA) cycle, developed by Dr. W. Edwards Deming, remains one of the most effective tools for improving safety processes. Its strength lies in its simplicity and repeatability:

1. Plan: Identify risks, set objectives, and design processes.
2. Do: Implement the plan at a small scale or pilot level.
3. Check: Measure outcomes, analyze results, and identify gaps.
4. Act: Adjust processes, standardize successful practices, and restart the cycle.

The PDCA cycle reinforces that safety is never "finished." It must be revisited constantly, adapting to new risks, technologies, and organizational realities.

- Aviation example: Airlines use PDCA to refine flight-deck checklists based on incident reports.

- Defense example: Weapons-loading procedures are improved by planning new steps, piloting them in a squadron, checking for errors or delays, and acting to standardize safer practices.
- Healthcare example: Hospitals apply PDCA to reduce infection rates, making iterative improvements until outcomes improve.

Leaders who embrace the PDCA model humility and vigilance, reminding their teams that improvement is not a one-time task but a continuous journey.

Safety Management Systems (SMS): A Structured Approach

In industries like aviation, SMS is not optional; it is mandated because it provides a systematic way to integrate safety into daily operations. SMS is built on four pillars:

1. **Safety Policy**: Leadership commitment to safety as a non-negotiable core value.
2. Safety Risk Management: Identifying, analyzing, and mitigating hazards before they cause harm.
3. Safety Assurance: Monitoring, measuring, and continuously improving safety performance.
4. Safety Promotion: Training, communication, and building a safety culture.

Servant leadership plays a vital role in SMS. Without leaders who genuinely care for people, SMS risks becoming a burdensome paperwork system instead of a living one. But when leaders prioritize people, SMS becomes a practical framework for trust and vigilance.

- Aviation example: SMS guides airlines in creating hazard-reporting systems where pilots and mechanics can report issues without fear of retaliation.
- Healthcare example: Hospitals use SMS to track near-misses in patient care, ensuring that lessons are learned before tragedies occur.

An effective SMS is never about compliance alone; it is about weaving safety into the fabric of daily decision-making.

High Reliability Organization (HRO) Principles

High Reliability Organizations (HROs) operate in environments where failure could be catastrophic, yet they manage to achieve remarkable safety records. Examples include nuclear power plants, aircraft carriers, and air traffic control centers.

HROs succeed not because they eliminate error entirely but because they anticipate and adapt to it. They operate with five defining principles:

1. Preoccupation with Failure: Treating small anomalies as warnings of bigger issues.
2. Reluctance to Simplify: Resisting easy explanations and digging into root causes.
3. Sensitivity to Operations: Maintaining constant situational awareness across all levels.
4. Commitment to Resilience: Preparing to respond quickly and recover from setbacks.
5. Deference to Expertise: Allowing the most knowledgeable person, not just the highest-ranking, to make decisions in the moment.

These principles give safety leaders a mindset for navigating uncertainty.

- Military example: On an aircraft carrier, a junior deckhand can stop a launch if they see a hazard, an example of deference to expertise.
- Energy example: Nuclear power plants treat minor alarms as potential signals of larger failures, acting preemptively to maintain resilience.

HRO thinking keeps organizations humble, curious, and responsive, traits essential for long-term safety.

Integrating Tools into Leadership Practice

These frameworks, PDCA, SMS, and HRO, are not meant to sit on shelves. Their value lies in daily integration into leadership behavior:

- A leader might apply PDCA to refine a weapons-loading checklist in the military.
- SMS could guide a healthcare facility in systematically addressing near-miss events.
- HRO principles might help an airline crew treat a small maintenance anomaly as a signal to ground an aircraft before catastrophe.

When these tools are combined with servant leadership values, organizations shift from compliance-driven safety to proactive cultures of vigilance.

Technology as an Enabler, not a Replacement

Modern technology, artificial intelligence, automation, predictive analytics, and advanced monitoring offer new ways to enhance safety. But leaders must remember technology is an enabler, not a replacement for culture.

- Predictive analytics can identify patterns of risk.
- Automation can reduce human error in repetitive tasks.
- Digital reporting systems can streamline feedback loops.

Yet no system can replace human judgment, ethical decision-making, or trust. Leaders must ensure technology is implemented responsibly and framed as a tool that serves people, not replaces them.

Building a Leader's Toolkit

The Safety Leadership Academy encourages each leader to build a personal safety toolkit, blending proven frameworks with personal experience and organizational context.

This toolkit might include:

- The PDCA cycle is a guide for improvement.
- SMS for structured integration of safety.
- HRO principles for vigilance in high-risk situations.
- Personal leadership practices such as servant leadership, storytelling, and after-action reviews.

By carrying these tools and using them daily, leaders build resilient organizations capable of navigating the uncertainties of high-stakes environments.

Looking Ahead

With tools and frameworks in place, the next chapter will shift to case studies and applications. These real-world examples will demonstrate how proactive safety leadership transforms organizations across various industries, including aviation, defense, healthcare, and beyond.

Chapter 9:
Case Studies and Applications

Principles and frameworks gain meaning only when applied to real-world challenges. In this chapter, we examine case studies from high-stakes environments, including aviation, defense, healthcare, and beyond, to see how proactive leadership and culture transform safety outcomes. These examples highlight both successes and failures, reminding us of the fact that leadership decisions shape results in powerful ways.

Aviation: Transforming Cockpit Culture

In the 1970s, aviation faced a troubling trend: many accidents were caused not by mechanical failure but by communication breakdowns in the cockpit. Hierarchical norms often silenced co-pilots. Even when they saw a captain making a dangerous decision, they hesitated to speak up.

One of the most tragic examples was the 1977 Tenerife disaster, where two Boeing 747s collided on the runway, killing 583 people. Investigations showed that deference to authority and unclear communication played central roles.

The introduction of Crew Resource Management (CRM) marked a turning point. CRM trained pilots to value input from every crew member, breaking down barriers of rank. Captains were taught to invite challenges, and co-pilots were empowered to speak. This shift reflected servant leadership principles, leaders serving the team by making space for every voice.

The results were dramatic. Accident rates fell, reporting improved, and aviation became one of the safest forms of transportation. CRM remains a prime example of how leadership and communication reshape culture, turning compliance into proactive vigilance.

Defense: Checklist Discipline in Weapons Loading

In military aviation, loading weapons is a high-risk, high-stakes task. A single mistake can endanger lives, compromise missions, or trigger international incidents. The Defense Contract Management Agency (DCMA) has long emphasized the importance of checklist discipline, verifying each step, validating processes, and holding teams accountable.

Yet checklists alone do not ensure safety. Leaders must model respect for the process. When commanders rush crews or dismiss procedures, errors multiply. When leaders embody servant leadership, listening to their teams, addressing fatigue, and ensuring discipline, checklists become living tools, not just paperwork.

One unit demonstrated this when leaders introduced daily safety huddles before operations. These meetings gave crews space to voice concerns about weather, equipment, or fatigue. Leaders responded by removing obstacles adjusting timelines, rotating assignments, or escalating issues to higher command. Mishaps dropped significantly, not because procedures changed, but because culture shifted. Leaders stopped directing and started serving, creating an environment where discipline and vigilance thrived.

Healthcare: Preventing Surgical Errors

Operating rooms mirror many of the dynamics of cockpits and combat zones. High stress, complex systems, and steep hierarchies create risk. Historically, nurses and anesthesiologists hesitate to question surgeons, even when they spot mistakes.

The introduction of surgical safety checklists, inspired by aviation, has begun to change outcomes. But the true transformation occurred when leaders adopted the servant leadership approach. Surgeons who began each operation with a "time out," a structured pause where every team member could confirm the patient, procedure, and plans, set the tone for psychological safety.

In one hospital, surgical complications dropped nearly 40% after structured communication was combined with leadership practices that encouraged openness. The difference was not the checklist alone, but the culture leaders created around it. When teams were invited to speak, they did, and lives were saved.

Energy: Learning from Nuclear Power

The nuclear industry offers lessons in both failure and resilience. The Chernobyl disaster (1986) revealed the cost of authoritarian cultures where fear silenced dissent. Operators followed unsafe instructions and ignored warnings because leadership discouraged questioning. The result was catastrophic.

By contrast, modern nuclear plants operate with High Reliability Organization (HRO) principles. Small anomalies are treated as potential signs of larger problems, and decision-making often defers to the person with the most technical expertise, not the highest rank. This cultural shift from control to collaboration demonstrates how servant leadership principles align with technical systems to create reliability under pressure.

Common Threads Across Industries

Though aviation, defense, healthcare, and energy operate in different domains, their lessons converge:

- Leadership sets the tone. Servant leaders foster cultures where safety is valued above hierarchy or convenience.
- Communication saves lives. Empowering every voice prevents small errors from escalating into tragedies.
- Checklists require culture. Tools work only when leaders reinforce their meaning and importance.
- Proactive systems outperform reactive ones. Organizations that anticipate risks through reporting, huddles, or near-miss analysis consistently perform better than those that wait for accidents.

These threads confirm that leadership and culture, not technology alone, are the decisive factors in safety.

Failures as Teachers

Not all case studies are about success. Some of the most powerful lessons come from failure.

- The Challenger disaster (1986) showed what happens when organizational culture suppresses dissent. Engineers raised concerns about O-ring seals in cold weather, but leadership prioritized schedule over safety. The shuttle launched and exploded.
- The Columbia disaster (2003) repeated the pattern. Foam damage was reported but dismissed. Leaders underestimated the risks, and the shuttle disintegrated on reentry.

These tragedies remind us that failure is rarely technical alone. Culture, communication, and leadership failures create the conditions for catastrophe.

Learning from failure is itself a hallmark of servant leadership. Leaders who acknowledge mistakes, share lessons, and adapt create resilience. Those who deny failure repeat history.

Applying Lessons to Your Organization

The Academy model invites leaders not to admire these examples from afar but to apply them locally. Questions to ask include:

Q1, Do we encourage every team member to speak up without fear?

Q2, Do leaders consistently model respect for processes and people?

Q3, Do we treat failures as punishments or as lessons?

Q4, Do our tools (checklists, reporting systems, training) support culture, or do they substitute for it?

By answering these questions honestly, leaders can assess their organization's current standing and chart a path toward proactive safety.

Looking Ahead

The case studies make one truth clear: leadership and culture determine safety. The next chapter will focus on measuring safety leadership effectiveness because what gets measured gets improved. Leaders must not only model values but also track whether those values are producing tangible results.

Chapter 10:
Measuring Safety Leadership Effectiveness

In high-stakes environments, leadership is often the hidden force behind safety outcomes. Policies, procedures, and technology matter, but the choices leaders make daily often determine whether safety is prioritized or compromised. Yet what is not measured is rarely improved.

If leaders want to strengthen proactive safety cultures, they must be able to measure their own effectiveness. Metrics provide visibility, reveal blind spots, and ensure accountability. But not all measures capture what matters. To truly evaluate safety leadership, organizations must look beyond compliance checklists and injury logs and instead measure the health of culture itself.

The Limits of Traditional Metrics

Most organizations rely heavily on lagging indicators such as:

- Number of accidents or incidents
- Lost-time injuries
- OSHA recordables
- Insurance claims

While these metrics are important, they reflect outcomes only *after something has gone wrong.* They are reactive by nature, telling leaders what has already happened rather than what is likely to happen.

For example, a plant may go months without an accident and appear "safe" on paper, yet this could mask a culture where hazards go unreported, and employees are afraid to speak up. Lagging indicators measure the absence of accidents, not the presence of trust or vigilance.

To improve safety leadership, organizations must balance lagging indicators with leading measures that show whether the right cultural conditions are in place.

Leading Indicators of Safety Leadership

Effective measurement requires shifting the focus toward leading indicator measures that predict future performance and reflect the influence of leadership. Examples include:

- **Reporting Rates:** Frequency of hazard reports, near-miss submissions, and safety suggestions. High reporting rates usually signal trust in leadership; low rates often indicate fear or apathy.

- **Participation Levels:** Attendance and engagement in safety briefings, huddles, and training programs. Genuine engagement, not just presence, signals leadership credibility.

- **Response Time:** How quickly leaders act on safety concerns and communicate resolutions. Delayed responses erode trust; fast, transparent responses strengthen it.

- **Observation Data:** Results from leadership walkarounds, peer-to-peer observations, and field audits. The presence of leaders in operations communicates commitment.

- **Employee Perceptions:** Survey data that capture beliefs such as "My leaders prioritize safety over production." These insights connect leadership actions directly to cultural impact.

For example, an oil refinery found that a spike in near-miss reports was not a sign of worsening conditions, but a breakthrough in culture: employees finally trusted leadership enough to speak up.

Cultural Assessments

Culture itself can and should be measured. Tools such as safety culture surveys, focus groups, and structured interviews provide insight into the values, norms, and behaviors shaping the workplace.

Key questions might include:

Q1, Do you feel safe reporting errors without fear of blame?

Q2, Do leaders act on safety concerns raised by employees?

Q3, Do you believe management values safety as much as productivity?

Q4, Would you stop a task if you believed it was unsafe?

The answers provide a mirror for leadership. Servant leaders embrace this feedback, even when it stings, using it as a roadmap for growth. Leaders who dismiss cultural assessments risk blind spots that undermine long-term performance.

Balanced Scorecards for Safety Leadership

One way to bring together metrics is through a balanced scorecard approach. This integrates lagging, leading, and cultural measures into a single view:

- **Lagging:** Injury rates, incident costs, equipment downtime.
- **Leading:** Near-miss reports, safety training completion, safety walk frequency.
- **Cultural:** Employee trust in leadership, confidence in reporting, perception of fairness.

For example, a manufacturing firm might track declining injury rates alongside increasing near-miss reporting and higher employee survey scores. Taken together, these measures show not only safer outcomes but also a healthier culture.

Balanced scorecards prevent organizations from chasing low numbers at the expense of openness and trust.

Accountability Through Transparency

Measurement means little without action. Leaders must share results with their teams to reinforce transparency and accountability.

When employees see leaders tracking safety performance, admitting shortcomings, and outlining corrective actions, credibility grows. A culture of accountability emerges not through punishment but through honesty.

- **Positive example:** An airline safety leader publishes monthly dashboards showing hazards reported, actions taken, and outcomes achieved.
- **Negative example:** A company that hides incident data fosters suspicion, rumor, and disengagement.

Transparency builds trust, which in turn fuels the very reporting and vigilance leaders seek.

Stories Beyond Numbers

Metrics are vital, but numbers alone never tell the whole story. They must be balanced with narratives.

- A rise in near-miss reports may sound alarming, but when paired with stories of employees speaking up without fear, it reflects progress.
- A decline in lost-time injuries could mean safer conditions, or it could mean employees are hiding injuries to avoid retaliation.

Stories bring data to life, revealing context and meaning. Lessons learned, after-action reviews, and employee testimonies give leaders the insight they need to interpret numbers correctly.

Leadership Reflection

Ultimately, measuring safety leadership is not just about dashboards or surveys, it is about reflection. Servant leaders regularly ask themselves:

Q1, Am I modeling the safety behaviors I expect?

Q2, Do I consistently listen and act when my people raise concerns?

Q3, Am I serving others, or am I expecting others to serve me?

Q4, Do my daily actions reinforce safety as a value, or do they send mixed signals?

Q5, Metrics provide evidence. Reflection provides wisdom. Together, they ensure leaders not only know the state of their culture but also understand their role in shaping it. Below is a Sample of a Safety Leadership scorecard to use in your organization.

Sample Safety Leadership Scorecard

The Safety Leadership Scorecard blends lagging, leading, and cultural indicators into a practical tool for assessing effectiveness. It gives leaders a balanced view not just of outcomes, but of the culture and proactive behaviors that shape them.

1. Lagging Indicators (Outcomes After Events)

These show historical performance. They must be monitored, but they are not enough on their own.

Metric	Example Target	Interpretation
Recordable injuries (OSHA/industry standard)	Year-over-year reduction	Declining rates show fewer incidents, but alone may mask underreporting.
Lost-time injuries	< 1 per 200,000 work hours	High numbers indicate serious safety issues; low numbers may reflect either safety success or a culture of silence.
Incident costs/claims	Trending downward	Financial impact is important, but should not be the sole measure of success.

2. Leading Indicators (Predictive Measures)

These measure proactive behaviors and predict future outcomes.

Metric	Example Target	Interpretation
Near-miss reports	20% increase YoY	A rise is usually positive; it shows growing trust in leadership. A drop may indicate fear or apathy.
Hazard identification reports	At least 2 per employee per quarter	Higher rates reflect vigilance and engagement.
Safety walkarounds by leaders	Weekly minimum	Leadership presence builds trust and visibility.
Response time to safety concerns	< 48 hours	Fast, transparent responses show respect and reinforce a reporting culture.

3. Cultural Indicators (Perceptions and Trust)

These measure the "invisible safety system," the values and norms driving behavior.

Metric	Example Target	Interpretation
Employee survey: "I feel safe reporting errors"	≥ 90% positive	High confidence signals psychological safety. Low scores reflect fear of blame.
Employee survey: "Leadership values safety over production"	≥ 85% positive	Aligns directly with servant leadership.
Participation in safety huddles/briefings	≥ 95% attendance, active input	Shows engagement; passive attendance is not enough.
Focus group themes	N/A	Qualitative feedback provides depth beyond numbers.

4. Storytelling and Lessons Learned (Narratives)

Numbers must be paired with stories that give them meaning.

Tool	Application	Leadership Action
After-action reviews	Conducted after every incident and near miss	Share lessons transparently with teams.
Case studies from within the organization	Used in quarterly training	Turn mistakes into learning opportunities.
Employee testimonials	Shared in briefings/newsletters	Reinforce positive behaviors and celebrate vigilance.

Using the Scorecard

1. Review across categories. Don't rely on lagging data alone; compare trends across leading and cultural measures.
2. Look for alignment. If lagging numbers are low but reporting rates are also low, the culture may be unhealthy.
3. Communicate results. Share openly with teams to build transparency and accountability.
4. Adapt targets. Numbers should be living benchmarks, refined as culture matures.

Example Application

- A defense unit reports fewer mishaps but also a drop in near-miss reports. The scorecard reveals the issue: crews may be staying silent. Leaders respond by holding, listening to sessions, reassuring teams, and rewarding hazard reporting.
- A hospital sees increased hazard reports and improved survey results alongside steady injury rates. While outcomes are flat, culture is improving, indicating stronger resilience over time.

The scorecard shows leaders what raw outcome data cannot: whether trust, vigilance, and culture are healthy beneath the surface.

Thoughts

A Safety Leadership Scorecard is not about chasing numbers; it is about reinforcing culture. When leaders track lagging, leading, and cultural measures together, they gain a holistic view of safety performance. More importantly, they send a clear message: *people matter, and leadership is accountable.*

Looking Ahead

With effectiveness measured, leaders must focus on sustaining growth. Data, stories, and reflection show where progress is being made and where gaps remain. The next chapter will explore how continuous learning and development ensure that safety leadership endures over time so that today's progress becomes tomorrow's standard.

Chapter 11:
Continuous Learning and Development

Safety leadership is not a destination; it is a continuous journey. High-stakes environments evolve constantly, new technologies emerge, regulations shift, missions change, and workforces diversify. Leaders who stop learning fall behind, and organizations that fail to adapt grow vulnerable. Sustaining proactive safety cultures requires leaders who are committed to ongoing learning, development, and resilience.

Why Continuous Learning Matters

Accidents often occur when organizations grow complacent. Past successes create a false sense of security, leading teams to relax vigilance. This "normalization of deviance," accepting risky shortcuts because nothing bad has happened yet, has preceded some of history's greatest disasters.

Continuous learning prevents stagnation by keeping leaders and teams alert, adaptable, and growth-oriented. In practice, continuous learning means:

- Updating knowledge and skills regularly. Regulations, technologies, and hazards change quickly. Leaders must stay current.
- Reflecting on successes and failures. After-action reviews and debriefs ensure lessons are captured, not forgotten.
- Seeking feedback. Employees and peers often see risks leaders miss.
- Tracking industry trends and emerging risks. From cyber threats to climate-driven hazards, staying informed is a form of vigilance.

Leaders who embrace lifelong learning signal to their teams that safety is dynamic, not static, and demands constant attention.

The Leader as Learner

Servant leaders model humility by showing they do not have all the answers. Instead, they approach challenges with curiosity and openness. This posture builds trust: when leaders are willing to learn, employees feel empowered to do the same. Leaders can demonstrate learning by:

- Sharing lessons from mistakes publicly. When a leader says, "Here's what I learned from this error," it normalizes honesty.
- Attending training sessions alongside employees. This reinforces that safety is everyone's responsibility.
- Asking open-ended questions. Phrases like "What are we missing?" or "What could go wrong?" encourage diverse input.
- Welcoming diverse perspectives. Cultural, generational, and experiential differences enrich decision-making.
- By positioning themselves as learners first and leaders second, they reinforce a culture where growth and adaptability are seen as strengths, not weaknesses.

Training and Development Programs

Structured development programs are vital for sustaining safety leadership. They should go beyond technical training to include human factors, leadership skills, and cultural awareness.

- Ongoing Training: Workshops on risk assessment, error management, and leadership communication.

- Simulations and Drills: Practicing emergencies—fires, equipment failures, cyberattacks builds muscle memory under pressure.
- Cross-Industry Learning: Borrowing from aviation, defense, and healthcare ensures broad adaptability.
- Certification and Accreditation: Professional designations (e.g., CSP, CSEP, NEBOSH) keep leaders aligned with global best practices.
- The most effective programs blend classroom instruction with experiential learning, ensuring knowledge translates into practice.

Coaching and Mentorship

Mentorship is one of the most powerful ways to sustain leadership development. Experienced leaders guide emerging ones, passing on not only technical knowledge but also cultural values.

- Coaching provides accountability. Leaders reflect on decisions, blind spots, and alignment with servant leadership principles.
- Mentorship ensures continuity. When senior leaders retire or move on, their wisdom lives on in those they mentored.
- Peer mentoring broadens growth. Leaders can learn as much from colleagues in other departments as they can from superiors.
- Organizations that institutionalize mentorship build resilience. They ensure that leadership values and lessons are not tied to individuals but embedded in the organization.

Organizational Learning

Continuous development must also be organizational, not just individual. High-reliability organizations (HROs) create formal structures to capture and share knowledge:

- Incident Reviews: Transparent analysis of accidents and near misses prevents repetition.
- Knowledge Sharing Platforms: Digital hubs where employees document hazards, fixes, and lessons learned.
- Learning Cultures: Rewarding curiosity and innovation instead of punishing experimentation.

For example, the U.S. Navy's nuclear program maintains its stellar safety record through rigorous knowledge transfer; each generation inherits lessons learned from the last. This continuity prevents the loss of institutional memory, one of the greatest risks in safety-critical fields.

Building Resilience Through Learning

Continuous learning is also about resilience, the ability to adapt and recover quickly from setbacks.

- Resilient organizations do not see failure as an endpoint but as an opportunity to learn.
- Resilient leaders encourage teams to experiment safely, knowing mistakes will generate growth.
- Resilient cultures bounce back stronger after crises because they capture and apply lessons.

By embedding resilience into learning systems, organizations ensure that setbacks do not derail progress but instead become stepping stones toward greater safety.

The Future of Safety Leadership Development

The future will demand new forms of learning:

- Digital Tools: Virtual simulations, e-learning, and real-time dashboards will enhance training. For example, VR can immerse workers in emergency scenarios, preparing them without real-world risk.
- Artificial Intelligence: AI can analyze near-miss reports and predict trends, helping leaders focus on emerging hazards.
- Globalization: Diverse, multicultural workforces require leaders to build cultural competency and understand how communication styles, risk perceptions, and decision-making vary across cultures.
- Hybrid Work Environments: As remote operations increase, leaders will need new strategies to maintain communication, engagement, and trust across digital platforms.

Even with these innovations, one truth remains: technology cannot replace leadership. Servant leaders must ensure digital tools enhance human judgment rather than substitute for it.

Looking Ahead

Continuous learning ensures safety cultures do not stagnate but evolve with the times. It keeps leaders humble, teams adaptable, and organizations resilient. The final chapter will look at the horizon, exploring how emerging challenges, technologies, and global pressures will shape the leaders of tomorrow, and how safety leadership must continue evolving in an uncertain world.

Chapter 12:
The Future of Safety Leadership

The challenges of tomorrow will test safety leaders in new and unprecedented ways. Advances in technology, shifts in workforce demographics, and global interdependence will reshape how organizations operate in high-stakes environments. Leaders who cling to outdated methods will struggle. Those who embrace change grounded in servant leadership and proactive culture will guide their organizations through uncertainty with resilience and vision.

Technology and Automation

Artificial intelligence, robotics, and automation are transforming industries at an accelerating pace.

- Aviation: Autonomous systems assist pilots with navigation, weather detection, and collision avoidance.

- Healthcare: AI algorithms help detect disease earlier and guide treatment decisions.

- Defense: Drones and unmanned systems carry out reconnaissance and even combat missions.

These technologies offer tremendous opportunities for enhanced safety Machines can handle repetitive, hazardous, or data-intensive tasks with precision. But they also introduce new risks:

- Over-reliance on automation can lead to complacency and skill degradation.

- Automation bias may cause operators to trust flawed systems without verification.

- Cyber vulnerabilities open new frontiers for threats that can bypass traditional safety defenses.

Future leaders must strike a balance between trusting technology and trusting people. Automation should never become a crutch. Training must keep human judgment sharp, ensuring that humans remain capable of intervening when machines fail.

The lesson is timeless: technology can support culture, but it cannot replace it.

Globalization and Cultural Diversity

Organizations increasingly operate across borders, managing teams with diverse cultural, generational, and social backgrounds. Safety leadership in this context requires cultural competence, the ability to understand, respect, and adapt to different perspectives.

- A pilot in Asia may hesitate to question a captain out of cultural deference to authority.
- A healthcare worker from a collectivist culture may prioritize team harmony over speaking up.
- A younger digital-native engineer may prefer instant messaging for reporting hazards, while an older colleague expects face-to-face dialogue.

Servant leadership provides the foundation for bridging these divides. By prioritizing people, listening with humility, and respecting differences, leaders create inclusive cultures where every voice matters. This inclusivity strengthens safety by ensuring that no perspective is dismissed because of culture, age, or status.

Climate, Sustainability, and Safety

Global pressures such as climate change, environmental sustainability, and resource scarcity will increasingly shape the mission of safety leadership.

- Extreme weather events like hurricanes, wildfires, and floods threaten operations and supply chains.

- Regulatory demands will force organizations to integrate environmental sustainability with safety systems.
- Resource scarcity will challenge leaders to manage risks while balancing economic pressures.

Future safety leaders must consider not only immediate hazards but also long-term environmental risks. Protecting people and protecting the planet will become interconnected missions. Safety leadership and sustainability leadership are converging, requiring leaders to think systemically about how human safety and environmental stewardship reinforce one another.

Generational Shifts in the Workforce

The workforce of the future will span multiple generations: Baby Boomers nearing retirement, Gen Xers in senior roles, Millennials in management, and Gen Z entering with digital-first mindsets.

- Younger employees often value transparency, adaptability, and purpose-driven work.
- Older employees bring wisdom, historical context, and long-cultivated expertise.

Leaders must integrate these strengths while managing generational friction. Servant leadership offers the answer: treating every individual with dignity, valuing contributions across age groups, and creating opportunities for collaboration and knowledge transfer.

For example, pairing seasoned experts with younger digital innovators in cross-generational mentoring creates resilience, ensuring that lessons of the past inform the technologies of the future.

High-Stakes Environments of Tomorrow

While aviation, defense, and healthcare will remain critical domains, new high-stakes environments are emerging:

- Cybersecurity is where digital attacks can compromise national security, economic stability, and human safety.
- Space operations, such as commercial ventures and exploration, expand risk into orbit and beyond.
- Critical infrastructure, including energy grids, water systems, and communications networks, is increasingly under threat from both physical and cyber disruptions.

Safety leadership principles, servant leadership, PDCA, SMS, and HRO practices remain consistent. But their applications will evolve. Leaders must adapt proven frameworks to these new frontiers, ensuring resilience in contexts where the consequences of failure are global and long-lasting.

The Unchanging Core: Servant Leadership

Despite technological advances, environmental pressures, and demographic shifts, one truth will endure: safety leadership begins and ends with people.

- Technology may predict risks, but it cannot build trust.
- Globalization may diversify teams, but only servant leaders can unify them.
- Climate change may alter missions, but leaders grounded in humility and service will keep human dignity at the forefront.

Servant leadership will remain the cornerstone because it transcends trends. By prioritizing people, listening actively, and empowering others, servant leaders create cultures that endure even as challenges change.

Preparing for the Next Generation of Leaders

The Safety Leadership Academy framework must not only guide today's leaders but also prepare them for tomorrow.

- Mentorship: Passing down lessons, wisdom, and values across generations.
- Training: Equipping leaders with technical skills, cultural competence, and adaptive thinking.
- Development pathways: Ensuring leaders are shaped not only by compliance requirements but also by exposure to complexity, uncertainty, and global perspectives.

The next generation must inherit more than procedures; they must inherit values of humility, accountability, and service.

Looking Beyond Today

The future of safety leadership will be complex, but the path is clear. Leaders who combine timeless principles with adaptive tools will shape cultures capable of thriving under pressure. As technology evolves and global challenges intensify, the need for leaders who serve, protect, and empower others will only grow.

The proactive safety cultures we build today are the foundation of tomorrow's resilience.

Conclusion:
A Call to Action for Safety Leaders

Safety is not an accident. It is the direct outcome of leadership, culture, and commitment. Across this book, we have seen that checklists, systems, and tools are only as strong as the leaders who put them into practice.

Technology may evolve, regulations may change, and industries may expand into new frontiers, but one truth remains constant: leadership shapes culture, and culture determines safety.

In high-stakes environments, leadership must be more than authority; it must be service. Servant leaders place people first, model humility, and create trust. They transform safety from a program into a way of life. They empower every voice, encourage transparency, and sustain vigilance even when pressure mounts.

The Safety Leadership Academy framework provides the foundation: competencies, tools, and practices to help leaders build proactive safety cultures. But frameworks alone do not change organizations; leaders do. Every choice you make, every conversation you have, and every behavior you model shapes the invisible system that governs your workplace.

The call is clear: safety leadership is not optional. It is the responsibility of every leader guiding people in environments where failure is not an option. Lives, missions, and futures depend on it.

Appendix: Safety Leadership Academy Competency Checklist

This checklist is designed as a quick reference for leaders seeking to assess and strengthen their own practice of safety leadership.

Core Competencies

☑ Servant Leadership

- Do I put people before processes and production?
- Do I listen actively and invite input from all team members?
- Do I empower others to take ownership of safety decisions?

☑ Systems Thinking

- Do I view safety as an interconnected system rather than isolated parts?
- Do I look beyond individual errors to examine organizational factors?

☑ Communication Mastery

- Do I create psychological safety where all voices can be heard?
- Do I use structured communication methods in both routine and crisis settings?
- Do I close feedback loops by acting on and reporting back about safety concerns?

☑ Decision-Making Under Pressure

- Do I remain calm and clear when the stakes are high?
- Do I balance short-term goals with long-term safety priorities?
- Do I involve the right expertise, not just the highest rank?

☑ Cultural Stewardship

- Do I model safety behaviors consistently?

- Do I reinforce a just culture where errors are learning opportunities?
- Do I hold myself accountable to the same standards as others?

☑ Learning Orientation

- Do I reflect on and share lessons from both successes and failures?
- Do I encourage continuous training and mentorship in my teams?
- Do I adapt to new risks, technologies, and workforce needs?

About the Author

Keric D. Craig, Ed.D., holds a Doctorate in Organizational Leadership and Development and a master's degree in aerospace/aviation safety systems. He currently serves as a Quality Engineer for one of the leading defense companies in the world, where he applies his expertise in safety systems and organizational leadership to mission-critical programs.

Before transitioning to the defense industry, Dr. Craig served 26 years in the United States Air Force, where he held multiple high-pressure leadership positions, including Nuclear Weapons Superintendent. In these roles, he was entrusted with the management of sensitive operations, the oversight of elite teams, and the maintenance of uncompromising safety standards under the most demanding conditions. His career in uniform provided him with firsthand experience in leading under pressure, shaping resilient organizations, and safeguarding missions of national consequence.

With experience in high-stakes environments, Dr. Craig has dedicated his career to building proactive safety cultures that protect people, advance missions, and sustain organizational excellence. His work bridges leadership theory and practical application, equipping leaders with the tools and values needed to thrive in complex and high-consequence industries.

References List

Columbia Accident Investigation Board. (2003). Columbia accident investigation board report. U.S. Government Printing Office.

Cullen, W. D. (1990). The public inquiry into the Piper Alpha disaster. Her Majesty's Stationery Office.

Deming, W. E. (1986). Out of the crisis. MIT Press.

Greenleaf, R. K. (2002). Servant leadership: A journey into the nature of legitimate power and greatness (25th Anniversary ed.). Paulist Press.

International Atomic Energy Agency. (1992). The Chernobyl accident: Updating of INSAG-1. Safety Series No. 75-INSAG-7. IAEA.

International Civil Aviation Organization. (1978). Report on the accident to KLM Flight 4805 and Pan American Flight 1736 at Tenerife Airport, Canary Islands, Spain on March 27, 1977. ICAO.

International Civil Aviation Organization. (2013). Safety management manual (SMM) (3rd ed.). ICAO Doc 9859.

National Aeronautics and Space Administration. (1967). Report of the Apollo 204 review board to the Administrator, NASA. U.S. Government Printing Office.

National Aeronautics and Space Administration. (1986). Report of the Presidential Commission on the Space Shuttle Challenger accident. U.S. Government Printing Office.

National Commission on the BP Deepwater Horizon Oil Spill and Offshore Drilling. (2011). Deep water: The Gulf oil disaster and the future of offshore drilling – Report to the President. U.S. Government Printing Office.

National Transportation Safety Board. (1990). Aircraft accident report: United Airlines flight 232, McDonnell Douglas DC-10-10, Sioux Gateway Airport, Sioux City, Iowa, July 19, 1989 (NTSB/AAR-90/06). NTSB.

National Transportation Safety Board. (1990). Grounding of the U.S. tankship Exxon Valdez on Bligh Reef, Prince William Sound near Valdez, Alaska, March 24, 1989 (NTSB Report No. MAR-90/04). U.S. Government Printing Office.

National Transportation Safety Board. (2010). Loss of thrust in both engines after encountering a flock of birds and subsequent ditching on the Hudson River, US Airways Flight 1549, Airbus A320-214, N106US, Weehawken, New Jersey, January 15, 2009 (NTSB/AAR-10/03). NTSB.

Nuclear Emergency Response Headquarters. (2011). Report of the Japanese Government to the IAEA Ministerial Conference on Nuclear Safety: The accident at TEPCO's Fukushima Nuclear Power Stations. Government of Japan.

Reason, J. (1997). Managing the risks of organizational accidents. Ashgate.

Roberts, K. H. (1990). Some characteristics of high-reliability organizations. Organization Science, 1(2), 160–177. https://doi.org/10.1287/orsc.1.2.160

Weick, K. E., & Sutcliffe, K. M. (2015). Managing the unexpected: Sustained performance in a complex world (3rd ed.). Wiley.

World Health Organization. (2009). WHO guidelines for safe surgery: Safe surgery saves lives. WHO Press.

Appendices

The following appendices are designed as quick-reference tools for safety leaders. Throughout the book, we explored real-world case studies and leadership frameworks in depth. These summaries bring the lessons together in a concise format that can be revisited in daily practice.

• Appendix A: Case Studies at a Glance highlights key events from aviation, defense, healthcare, and energy, showing how leadership decisions shaped outcomes. Each case distills the critical leadership lesson so future leaders can apply the insights without repeating past mistakes.

• Appendix B: Leadership Frameworks at a Glance organizes the core models and tools used across high-stakes industries. These frameworks provide practical methods for sustaining proactive safety cultures and guiding resilient organizations.

Leaders are encouraged to use these appendices as checklists, reminders, and conversation starters within their teams. Safety leadership is not only about remembering the past but applying its lessons to shape the future.

Appendix B: Leadership Frameworks at a Glance

Framework/Tool	Origin/Key Source	Core Principles	Leadership Lesson
Servant Leadership	Robert K. Greenleaf (1970s)	Prioritize people over processes; listen first, empower teams; model humility.	Leaders serve their people first; trust and safety grow when leaders put human well-being above production.
PDCA Cycle (Plan-Do-Check-Act)	W. Edwards Deming (1986)	Continuous improvement: plan solutions, implement, evaluate, adjust	Safety is never "finished"; improvement is ongoing, requiring humility and vigilance from leaders.
Safety Management Systems (SMS)	ICAO (2013)	Four pillars: safety policy, risk management, assurance, promotion	A systematic, organization-wide approach ensures safety is built into daily operations—not treated as an afterthought.
High Reliability Organization (HRO) Principles	Weick & Sutcliffe (2015); Roberts (1990)	Preoccupation with failure, reluctance to simplify, sensitivity to operations, commitment to resilience,	Complex systems succeed when leaders remain humble, anticipate risks, and empower the most knowledgeable

		deference to expertise	person—not just the highest rank.
Just Culture	James Reason (1997)	Distinguishes between human error, at-risk behavior, and reckless behavior	Balances accountability with trust; mistakes become learning opportunities instead of silenced failures.
Psychological Safety	Amy Edmondson (1999; extended in later research)	People feel safe to speak up, admit errors, and share concerns	Safety thrives when leaders remove fear and protect truth-tellers; silence kills.

www.ingramcontent.com/pod-product-compliance
Lightning Source LLC
Chambersburg PA
CBHW040908210326
41597CB00029B/5007